C000246340

Many many thanks!

Inspire Books is an imprint
of Peter Pauper Press, Inc.

For permissions please see the
last page of this book.

Text copyright © 1999
Peter Pauper Press, Inc.
202 Mamaroneck Avenue
White Plains, NY 10601
Illustrations copyright © Mary Russel
1989, 1990, 1991, 1993,
1994, 1995, 1998
All rights reserved
ISBN 0-88088-130-5
Printed in China
9 8 7

Visit us at www.peterpauper.com

A True
Friend is
a Gift
from God

A friend loves
at all times . . .

PROVERBS 17:17 NIV

*I*mitating Christ
is opening the door
to friendship.

BILLY GRAHAM

Greater love has no one than this, that he lay down his life for his friends.

JOHN 15:13 NIV

There are
deep sorrows
and killing cares
in life, but the
encouragement and
love of friends
were given us to
make all
difficulties
bearable.

JOHN OLIVER HOBBES

Some friendships are made by nature, some by contract, some by interest, and some by souls.

JEREMY TAYLOR

Years may wrinkle
the skin, but lack
of friendship will
wrinkle the soul.

Real friends are
those who, when
you make a fool
of yourself, don't
think you've done
a permanent job.

And a friend
once won, need never
be lost, if we will
only be trusty and
true ourselves.

CHARLES KINGSLEY

Moreover as for me,
God forbid that I should
sin against the LORD in
ceasing to pray for you:
but I will teach you
the good and the right way.

1 SAMUEL 12:23 KJV

A real friend will tell
you your faults and follies
in times of prosperity,
and assist you with
his hand and heart in
times of adversity.

Blessings come in
different shapes and sizes.
So do friends, because
friends are one of life's
best blessings.

I constantly
remember you
in my prayers
night and day.

2 TIMOTHY 1:3 NASB

Dear Lord, my friends
have been to me

Interpreters of love divine,

And in their kindness
I have seen

Thine everlasting
mercy shine!

And so I pray on this
Thy day,

That Thou wilt search
through gifts of Thine,

And choose Thy rarest,
fairest ones,

To shower upon these
friends of mine!

MARTHA SHELL NICHOLSON

For I have come
to have much joy
and comfort
in your love . . .

PHILEMON 7 NASB

Our Lord never inculcated
an isolated holy life. . . .
The Holy Spirit entering
into the personal spirit
instantly puts us into
affinity with every other
person in the light . . .

OSWALD CHAMBERS

The main business of friendship is to sustain and make bearable each other's burdens. We may do more of that as friends than we do anything else.

EUGENE KENNEDY

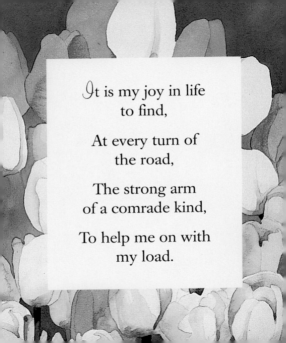

It is my joy in life
to find,

At every turn of
the road,

The strong arm
of a comrade kind,

To help me on with
my load.

And since I have
no gold to give,

And love alone must
make amends,

My only prayer is
while I live,

"God, make me worthy
of my friends!"

On sunny days,
you're my shade tree;

On cloudy days,
you're my sun;

On birthdays,
you're my candlelight;

On cheerless days,
you're such fun.

On wintry days,
you warm me up;

On summer days,
you're my breeze;

But most of all
on everyday;

You're the best
of friends to me.

SARAH MICHAELS

Let nothing therefore
hinder us, let nothing
separate us, let nothing
come between us.

FRANCIS OF ASSISI

I thank my God,
making mention
of thee always
in my prayers . . .

PHILEMON 4 KJV

Blessed are they who have the gift of making friends, for it is one of God's best gifts. It involves many things, but above all, the power of going out of one's self, and appreciating whatever is noble and loving in another.

THOMAS HUGHES

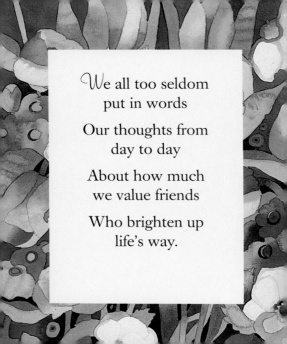

We all too seldom
put in words

Our thoughts from
day to day

About how much
we value friends

Who brighten up
life's way.

So this is just to
let you know

What's now and
always true:

All the best that
friendship means

Is centered right
in *you*.

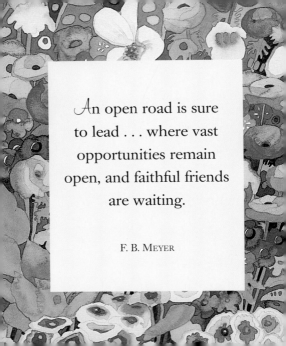

An open road is sure
to lead . . . where vast
opportunities remain
open, and faithful friends
are waiting.

F. B. MEYER

$\mathcal{A}$ true friend
is the gift of God,
and he only who made
hearts can unite them.

ROBERT SOUTH

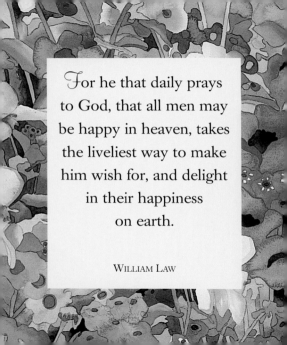

For he that daily prays
to God, that all men may
be happy in heaven, takes
the liveliest way to make
him wish for, and delight
in their happiness
on earth.

WILLIAM LAW

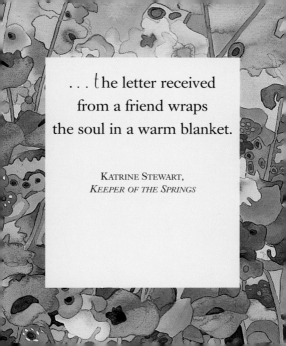

. . . the letter received
from a friend wraps
the soul in a warm blanket.

KATRINE STEWART,
KEEPER OF THE SPRINGS

You have put gladness
in my heart . . .

PSALMS 4:7 NKJV

. . . the pleasantness of
one's friend springs from
his earnest counsel.

PROVERBS 27:9 NIV

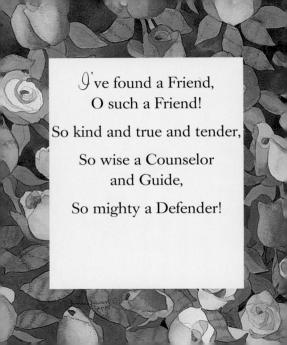

I've found a Friend,
O such a Friend!

So kind and true and tender,

So wise a Counselor
and Guide,

So mighty a Defender!

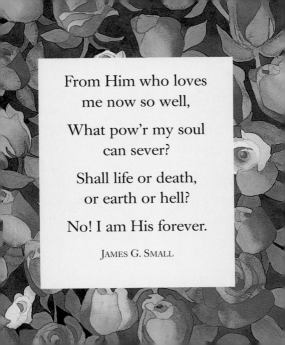

From Him who loves
me now so well,

What pow'r my soul
can sever?

Shall life or death,
or earth or hell?

No! I am His forever.

JAMES G. SMALL

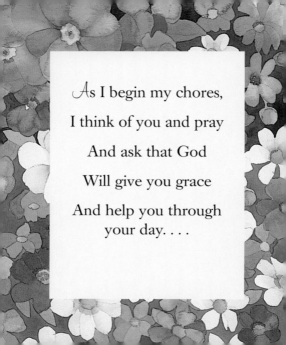

As I begin my chores,

I think of you and pray

And ask that God

Will give you grace

And help you through
your day. . . .

As I wind up my day,
And take my evening rest
I thank the Lord
For such a gift—
Friends bring such
happiness.

SARAH MICHAELS

*G*od has bound us so strongly to each other, that no man ought to endeavor to avoid subjection; and where love reigns, mutual services will be rendered.

JOHN CALVIN

$\mathcal{I}$ have learned that
to have a good friend
is the purest of all God's
gifts, for it is a love that
has no exchange
of payment.

FRANCES FARMER

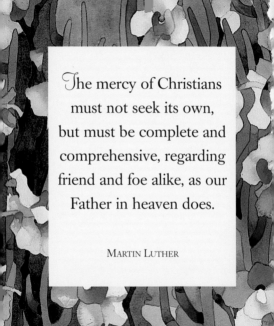

The mercy of Christians
must not seek its own,
but must be complete and
comprehensive, regarding
friend and foe alike, as our
Father in heaven does.

MARTIN LUTHER

True friendship is
like sound health;
the value of it is seldom
known until it be lost.

CHARLES CALEB COLTON

A true friend shares freely,
advises justly, assists readily,
adventures boldly, takes
all patiently, defends
courageously, and continues
a friend unchangeably.

WILLIAM PENN

What a Friend we have
in Jesus,

All our sins and griefs
to bear!

What a privilege to carry

Everything to God
in prayer!

Do thy friends despise,
forsake thee?

Take it to the Lord
in prayer;
In His arms He'll take
and shield thee,
Thou wilt find a solace there.

JOSEPH M. SCRIVEN

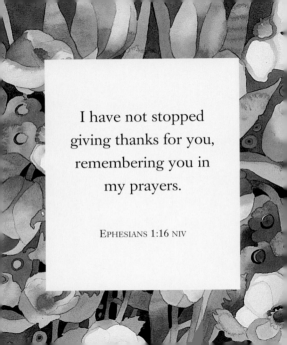

I have not stopped
giving thanks for you,
remembering you in
my prayers.

EPHESIANS 1:16 NIV

A man that hath friends
must shew himself friendly.

PROVERBS 18:24 KJV

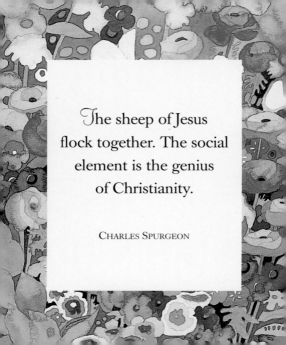

The sheep of Jesus
flock together. The social
element is the genius
of Christianity.

CHARLES SPURGEON

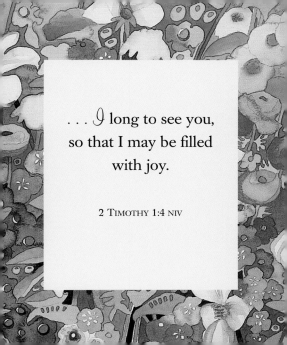

. . . *I* long to see you,
so that I may be filled
with joy.

2 TIMOTHY 1:4 NIV

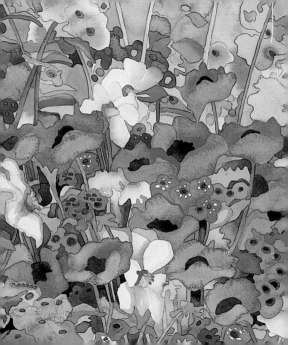

He who
clasps the hand
of a friend
holds tight to
a blessing.

A friend is one who knows you as you are, understands where you've been, accepts who you have become, and still gently invites you to grow.

A friend will joyfully
sing with you when you are
on the mountain top, and
silently walk beside you
through the valley.

One loving heart
sets another on fire.

AUGUSTINE

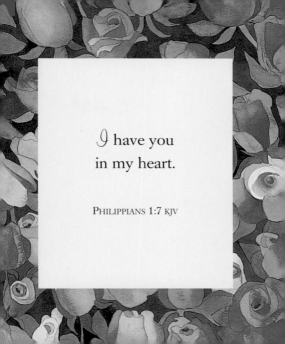

I have you
in my heart.

PHILIPPIANS 1:7 KJV

Even as David thanked God for Jonathan and praised him in well-remembered lines, so have we abundant reasons to thank God today for friends and to resolve to keep these friendships in constant repair.

EDGAR DeWITT JONES

$\mathcal{A}$ man must get friends
as he would get food
and drink for nourishment
and sustenance.

RANDOLPH BOURNE

The LORD bless you,
and keep you;

The LORD make His face
shine on you,

And be gracious to you;

The LORD lift up
His countenance on you,

and give you peace.

NUMBERS 6:24–26 NASB

True friendship is
a plant of slow growth.

GEORGE WASHINGTON

Wise is the man
who fortifies his life
with friendships.

A friend makes
the world a more
beautiful place to live.

God's best gifts
are often wrapped in the
love of our friends.

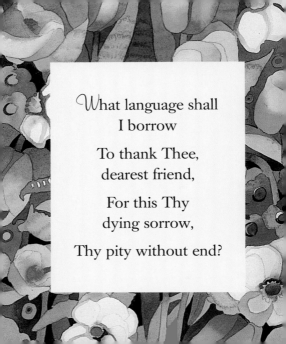

What language shall
I borrow

To thank Thee,
dearest friend,

For this Thy
dying sorrow,

Thy pity without end?

O make me Thine forever;

And should I fainting be,

Lord, let me never, never

Outlive my love to Thee.

Amen.

BERNARD OF CLAIRVAUX

Above all,
keep fervent in
your love for one
another, because love
covers a multitude
of sins.

1 Peter 4:8 NASB

The friend who
understands you,
creates you.

ROMAIN ROLLAND

Any good work,
kindness or service I can
render to any person . . . ,
let me do it now. Let me
not neglect or delay to
do it, for I will not pass
this way again.

AN OLD QUAKER SAYING

*I*t is prudent
to pour the oil
of delicate politeness
upon the machinery
of friendship.

COLETTE

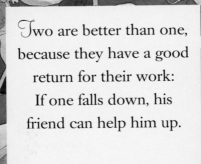

Two are better than one,
because they have a good
return for their work:
If one falls down, his
friend can help him up.

ECCLESIASTES 4:9–10 NIV

There are only
two people who can tell
you the truth about
yourself—an enemy who
has lost his temper
and a friend who loves
you dearly.

ANTISTHENES

Scripture quotations marked NASB are taken from the *New American Standard Bible.* Copyright © 1960, 1962, 1963, 1968, 1971, 1972, 1973, 1975, 1977 by The Lockman Foundation. Used by permission.

Scripture quotations marked NIV are taken from the *Holy Bible, New International Version*®. Copyright © 1973, 1978, 1984 by International Bible Society. Used by permission of Zondervan Publishing House. All rights reserved.

Scripture quotations marked KJV are taken from the *King James Version* of the Bible.

Scripture quotations marked NKJV are taken from *The New King James Version* of the Bible. Copyright © 1979, 1980, 1982, 1994 by Thomas Nelson, Inc., Publishers. Used by permission.